The Sebring Experience
Adult Coloring Book

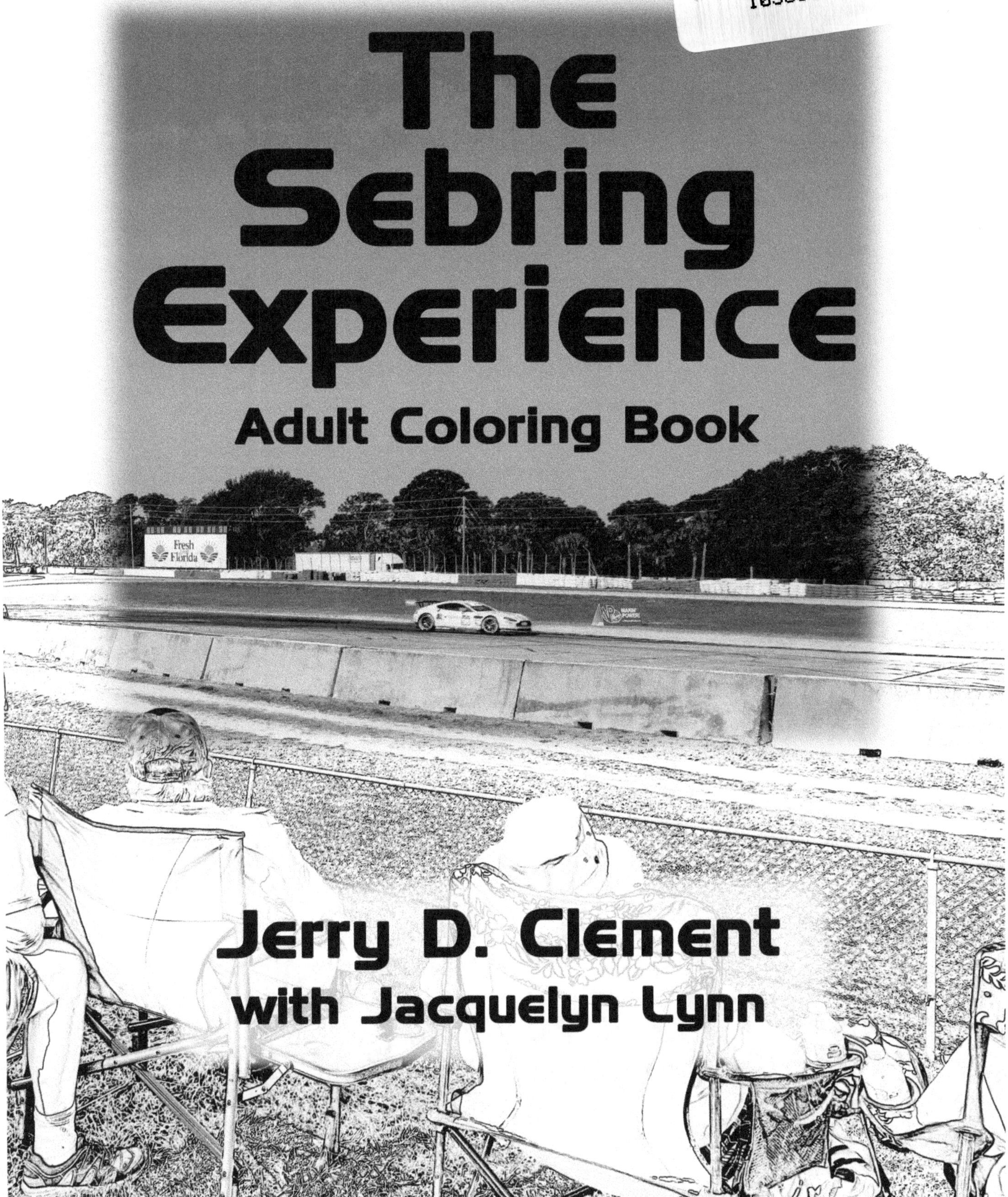

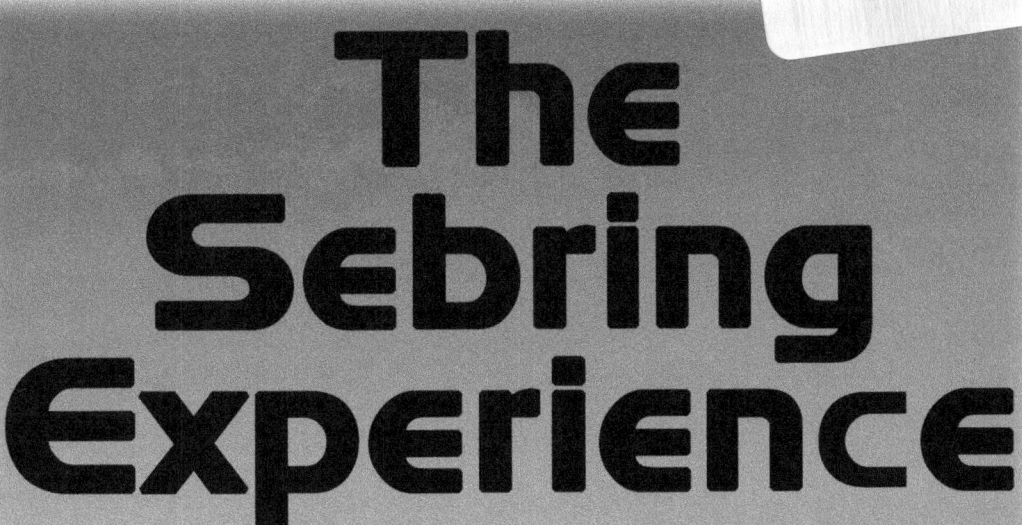

Jerry D. Clement

with Jacquelyn Lynn

Publisher: Tuscawilla Creative Services, LLC
Cover Design: Jerry D. Clement
Production and Composition: Tuscawilla Creative Services

Copyright © 2016 by Jerry D. Clement & Jacquelyn Lynn

All rights reserved. No part of this publication may be reproduced, distributed or transmitted in any form or by any means, without prior written permission.

Tuscawilla Creative Services, LLC
P. O. Box 1501
Goldenrod, FL 32733-1501

www.CreateTeachInspire.com

For bulk purchase information, email info@contacttcs.com

The Sebring Experience Adult Coloring Book / Jerry D. Clement & Jacquelyn Lynn

ISBN: 978-1-941826-12-6

Attending the 12 Hours of Sebring has been a tradition in our family for years. Planning begins shortly after Christmas for the four-day adventure that culminates in the world-famous 12-hour endurance race held annually on the third Saturday in March in south-central Florida. Our group arrives in multiple vehicles, ready as soon as the gates open to stake out a campsite that serves as our headquarters for all the prerace activities as well as the postrace celebration.

America's oldest road racing track, Sebring International Raceway, has a rich history. It was originally Hendricks Field, a World War II airbase used to train B-17 combat crews. After the war, aeronautical engineer, entrepreneur and car enthusiast Alec Ulmann organized a six-hour endurance race across the field's long, broad runways and network of access roads. That race was held on December 31, 1950, and we can only imagine what that New Year's Eve celebration was like. The first 12-hour race was held 15 months later on March 15, 1952.

The 3.74-mile concrete and asphalt track has been challenging the giants of sports car racing ever since in a grueling endurance test that is second only to Le Mans in international prestige.

In addition to its legendary reputation within the racing circuit, Sebring is also a celebrity magnet. Steve McQueen, James Brolin, Paul Newman, Gene Hackman, Lorenzo Lamas, David Carradine, Patrick Dempsey and even journalist Walter Cronkite have competed at Sebring.

Sebring has its share of macabre history as well. Notorious serial killer Christopher Wilder drove in the 1983 race, and one of the victims of the Charles Manson family in 1969 was Jay Sebring, a hair salon entrepreneur who was born Thomas Kummer but changed his name to that of the famous race because he liked the way it sounded. And the Ford GT in which driver Bob McLean was killed in a fiery crash in 1966 was buried at a nearby property.

Our experiences at Sebring include extreme heat, unusual cold, sun, rain and even huddling in the restroom (the only available brick building) while a tornado ripped through the camps. We've seen some phenomenal performances by drivers and their vehicles, met some unforgettable people and made lifelong memories.

In *The Sebring Experience* coloring book, we share some of that with you.

So … ladies and gentlemen, start your pencils. Let's color!

Jerry D. Clement

Thanks to Sebring International Raceway's website, www.sebringraceway.com, for providing much of the historical and statistical information shared here.

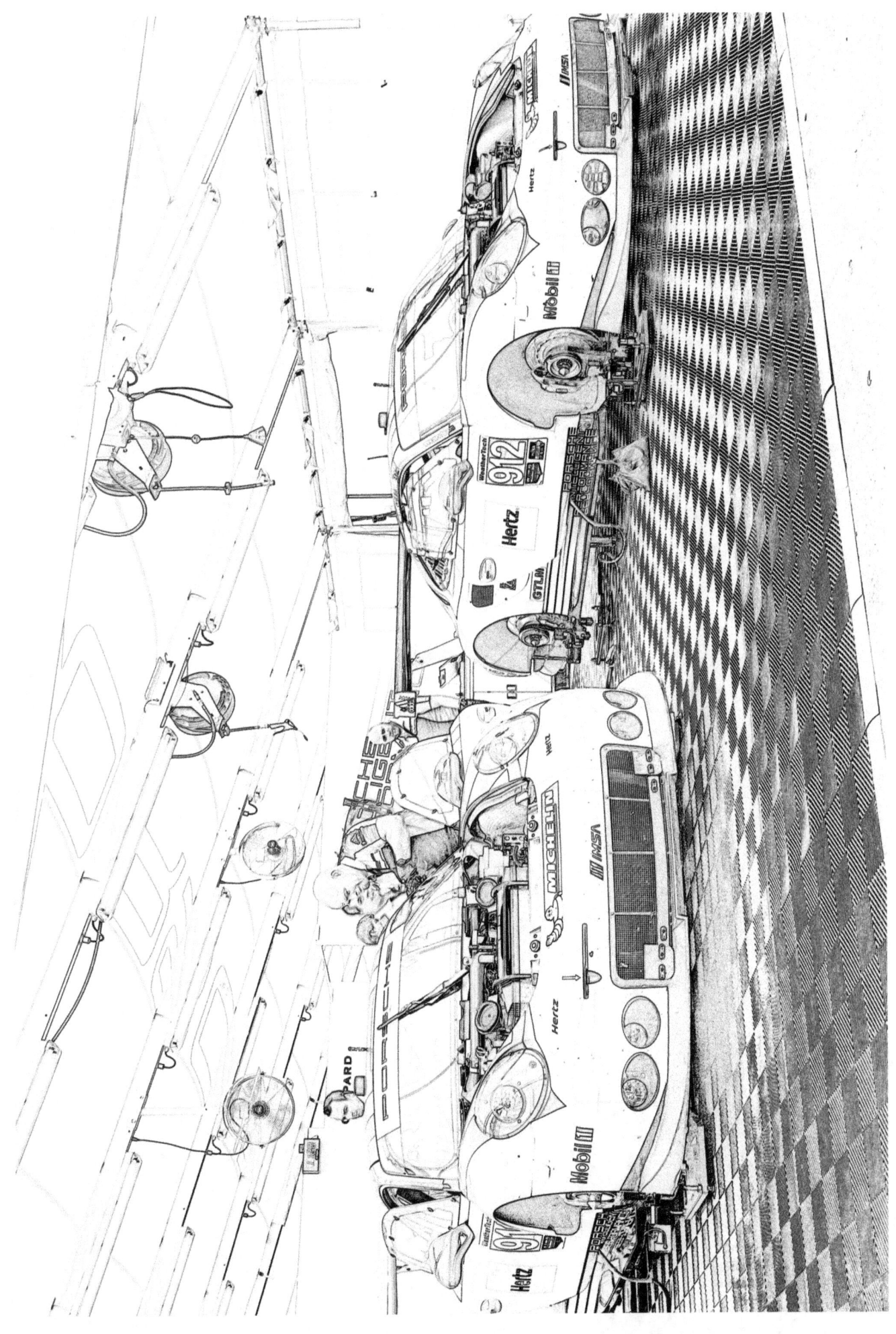

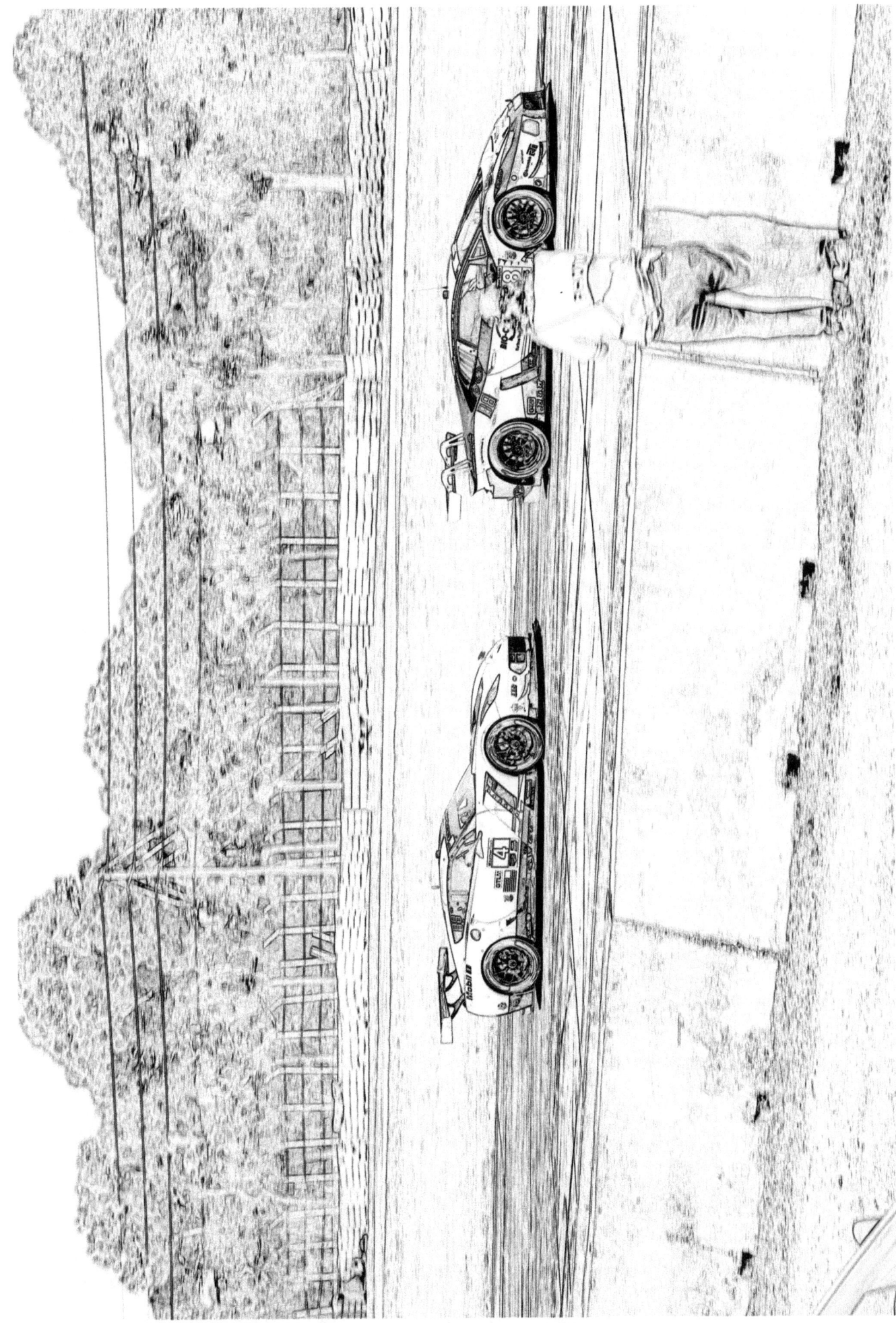

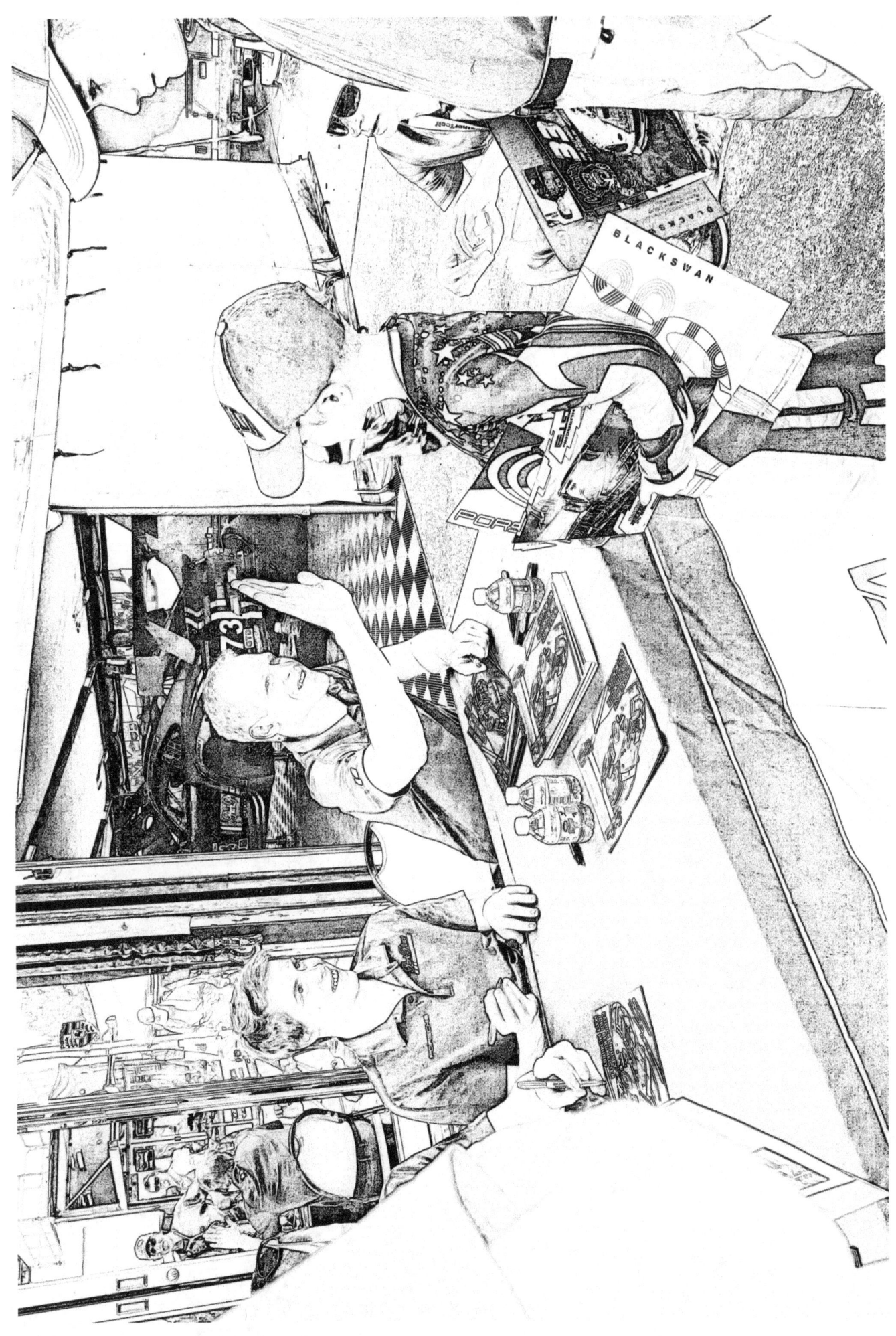

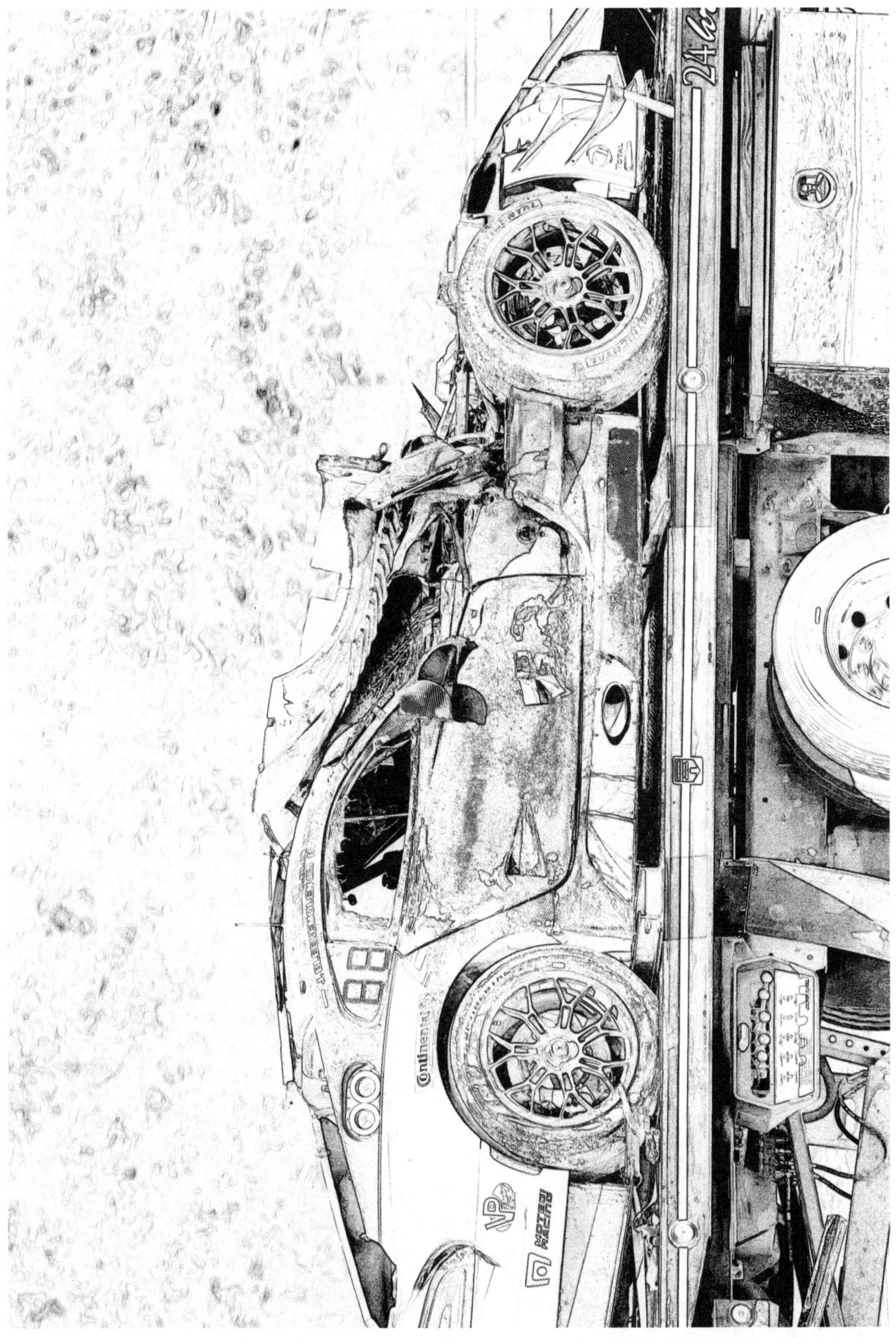

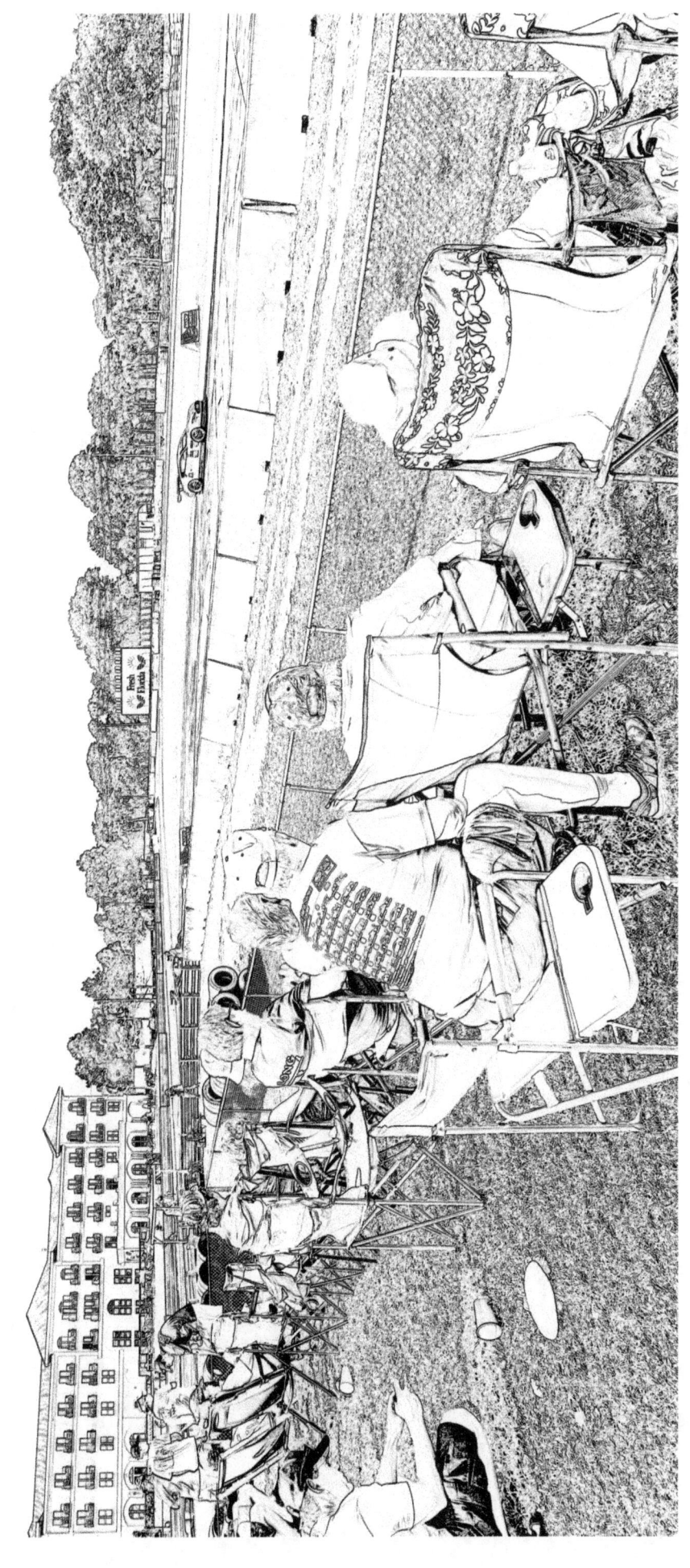

Also from Create! Teach! Inspire!

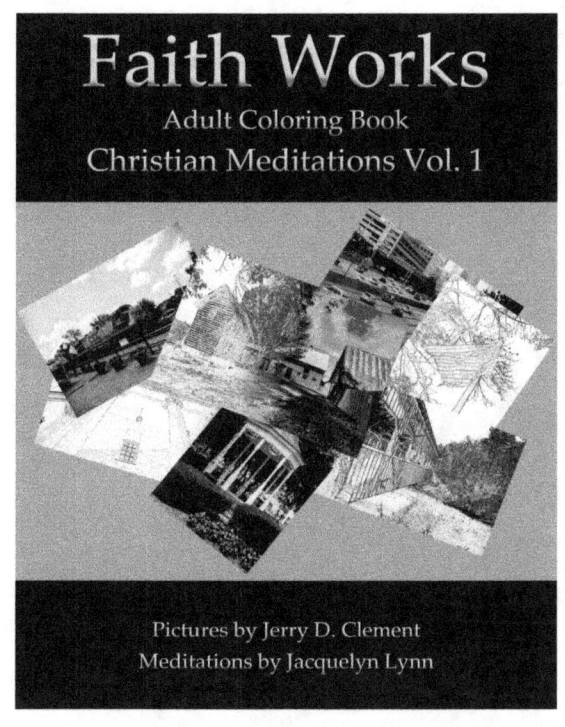 

For a complete list of available Faith Works Adult Coloring Books, visit **www.CreateTeachInspire.com/adult-coloring-books**.

As our thanks for your purchase, we'd like to give you five more images you can print and color.

Download them now at **www.CreateTeachInspire.com/color**.

Join our Facebook group at:
www.facebook.com/groups/relaxandcolor

More from Create! Teach! Inspire!

Faith Works
Images for Impact

Customizable images to energize your message on social media & websites

www.CreateTeachInspire.com

Faith Works **Images for Impact** are original images you can easily customize for use on your blog, website, social media and presentations using software you probably already have on your computer.

These beautiful, high-quality photographs by Jerry D. Clement are substantially more affordable than traditional stock photography. Each collection includes five themes (sets of images), complete instructions for how to create your own custom images, and access to video tutorials.

Visit **www.FaithWorksImages.com** to see our available collections and to order.

Words to Work By
31 devotions for the workplace based on the Book of Proverbs

Messages of inspiration and motivation based on the teachings of the world's greatest business advisor: King Solomon.

Our faith is a part of who we are, and we don't leave it at the door when we go to work. But sometimes in the mad chaos of today's business world, we need the peace, comfort and guidance that a brief devotion and prayer can bring.

Words to Work By provides those devotions and prayers.

Finding Joy in the Morning
You *can* make it through the night

This is not a self-help book, this is an I-can't-do-it-alone book.

Finding Joy in the Morning shows you how to surrender the natural human proclivity to try to be in control so that you will know the peace and find the joy that comes with knowing God is always with you and always in control. You'll learn how to face seemingly insurmountable challenges with strength and resilience, and enjoy incredible peace during some of life's toughest times.

The book includes a prayer and a "Your Turn" section at the end of each chapter. It's designed to be read individually or used as a group study.

Available in print and Kindle versions on Amazon.com.

For more information about books by Jacquelyn Lynn, visit CreateTeachInspire.com.

www.ingramcontent.com/pod-product-compliance
Lightning Source LLC
Chambersburg PA
CBHW081355080526
44588CB00016B/2504